A Note from
Mary Pope Osborne About the

MAGIC TREE HOUSE®
FACT TRACKERS

When I write Magic Tree House® adventures, I love including facts about the times and places Jack and Annie visit. But when readers finish these adventures, I want them to learn even more. So that's why my husband, Will, and my sister, Natalie Pope Boyce, and I write a series of nonfiction books that are companions to the fiction titles in the Magic Tree House® series. We call these books Fact Trackers because we love to track the facts! Whether we're researching dinosaurs, pyramids, Pilgrims, sea monsters, or cobras, we're always amazed at how wondrous and surprising the real world is. We want you to experience the same wonder we do—so get out your pencils and notebooks and hit the trail with us. You can be a Magic Tree House® Fact Tracker, too!

Mary Pope Osborne

Here's what kids, parents, and teachers have to say about the Magic Tree House® Fact Trackers:

"They are so good. I can't wait for the next one. All I can say for now is prepare to be amazed!" —Alexander N.

"I have read every Magic Tree House book there is. The [Fact Trackers] are a thrilling way to get more information about the special events in the story." —John R.

"These are fascinating nonfiction books that enhance the magical time-traveling adventures of Jack and Annie. I love these books, especially *American Revolution*. I was learning so much, and I didn't even know it!" —Tori Beth S.

"[They] are an excellent 'behind-the-scenes' look at what the [Magic Tree House fiction] has started in your imagination! You can't buy one without the other; they are such a complement to one another." —Erika N., mom

"Magic Tree House [Fact Trackers] took my children on a journey from Frog Creek, Pennsylvania, to so many significant historical events! The detailed manuals are a remarkable addition to the classic fiction Magic Tree House books we adore!" —Jenny S., mom

"[They] are very useful tools in my classroom, as they allow for students to be part of the planning process. Together, we find facts in the [Fact Trackers] to extend the learning introduced in the fictional companions. Researching and planning classroom activities, such as our class Olympics based on facts found in *Ancient Greece and the Olympics*, help create a genuine love for learning!" —Paula H., teacher

Magic Tree House®
Fact Tracker

PANDAS AND OTHER ENDANGERED SPECIES

A nonfiction companion to
Magic Tree House® #48:
A Perfect Time for Pandas

by Mary Pope Osborne
and Natalie Pope Boyce

illustrated by Sal Murdocca

A STEPPING STONE BOOK™
Random House 🏠 New York

The Magic Tree House Fact Tracker series was formerly known as the
Magic Tree House Research Guide series.

Visit us on the Web!
MagicTreeHouse.com
randomhouse.com/kids

Educators and librarians, for a variety of teaching tools, visit us at
RHTeachersLibrarians.com

Library of Congress Cataloging-in-Publication Data
Osborne, Mary Pope.
Pandas and other endangered species / by Mary Pope Osborne and Natalie
Pope Boyce ; illustrated by Sal Murdocca.
  p. cm. — (Magic tree house fact tracker)
"A nonfiction companion to Magic tree house, #48: A Perfect Time for Pandas"
Includes index.
ISBN 978-0-375-87025-5 (trade) — ISBN 978-0-375-97025-2 (lib. bdg.)
1. Giant panda—Juvenile literature. 2. Endangered species—Juvenile
literature. I. Boyce, Natalie Pope. II. Murdocca, Sal, ill. III. Title.
QL737.C27O827 2012 599.789—dc23 2011044370

Printed in the United States of America
10 9 8 7 6 5 4 3 2

For Ezra Harris Rosenberg,
with gratitude for his advice and support

Scientific Consultant:
BRANDIE SMITH, Senior Curator, National Zoo, Washington, D.C.

Education Consultant:
HEIDI JOHNSON, language acquisition and science education specialist, Bisbee, Arizona

With special thanks to the Random House team: Gloria Cheng; Mallory Loehr; Chelsea Eberly; Sal Murdocca, whose art really makes the books come alive; and our editor, Diane Landolf, who keeps the whole thing going with grace and humor.

PANDAS AND OTHER
ENDANGERED SPECIES

Contents

Dear Readers,

In <u>A Perfect Time for Pandas</u>, we visited giant pandas in Southwest China. A terrible earthquake struck, and we tried our best to help them out. We learned that giant pandas are an endangered species. Without protection, all pandas may someday disappear. This made us want to track more facts about them and about other animals that are at risk.

What we learned amazed us! Many animals, like elephants, tigers, and gorillas, are in danger. They're animals that we've always thought would be around forever!

We decided to find out all we could

about pandas and other endangered animals. We learned that it's up to people to help if we want animals to survive. People are working hard to do this. Just read what they're doing to save whooping cranes in the United States!

So now is the time to pull out your notebooks and become a fact tracker like us. With all the things you learn, someday you can help make the future a good one for all creatures great and small.

Jack
Annie

1

Pandas and Other Endangered Species

April 16, 1972, was a crazy day in Washington, D.C.

Outside the National Zoo, cars were lined up bumper to bumper. Twenty thousand people waited in long lines at the gates. All of this fuss was about two chubby little panda cubs named Hsing Hsing and Ling Ling. They had just arrived as gifts from the Chinese government.

At this time, there were no other pandas in the United States. Ling Ling and Hsing Hsing were so special, they came with their own bodyguards! The pandas became the most popular animals at the zoo. Over the years, millions of people visited them.

 Ling Ling was a female, and Hsing Hsing was a male.

Endangered Species

Ling Ling and Hsing Hsing came from the high mountain forests of China. These mountains are home to all giant pandas living in the wild. Pandas are a badly *endangered species*.

A species is *endangered* when its numbers have become so small that the species is at risk of becoming *extinct* (ex-STINKT), or dying out. Today only about 1,600 pandas remain in the wild.

A <u>species</u> is a group of plants or animals that are alike in certain ways.

It's not only pandas that are in trouble. All over the world, thousands of living things are in danger of disappearing forever.

Extinction

Animals and plants have been on earth for hundreds of millions of years. At first, extinction happened in natural ways. Volcanic eruptions, for example, sometimes lasted thousands or even millions of years. Over time, events like this caused the extinction of millions of species. The one most people know about is when dinosaurs disappeared about 65 million years ago.

Extinction is a natural process—it makes way for lots of new species. But humans are causing animals and plants to become extinct too quickly, and fewer new species are taking their place. Species are being lost so fast that many are gone before they've even been discovered!

Over 800 animal and plant species have become extinct in the past 500 years.

Habitat Destruction

Habitats are the places where certain plants and animals live. There are more

16

people on earth now than ever before. Because the human population keeps growing, people are changing the land. They are destroying the habitats of many species.

When their habitats are destroyed, animals can't find enough food or shelter.

Human development of wetlands, grasslands, and tropical forests causes habitat loss. The land is used for things like farming, logging, mining, factories, and housing.

Giant pandas once lived in forests throughout southern and eastern China. Now they live only in the mountains of central China. China has over a billion people—more than any other country in the world.

There are more than 7 billion people on the planet.

When people think of forests, they think of trees. Pandas live in bamboo forests, but bamboo is a type of grass. There are almost 1,500 species of bamboo

17

in forests around the world. Because people cut down many of the bamboo forests, pandas lost much of their habitat.

The bamboo cleared from this forest was mostly used for flooring.

Pollution and Climate Change

Pollution is harmful for all living things. Chemicals and waste such as oil, pesticides, or sewage pollute the soil, air, and water and put many species at risk.

Climate change is another problem. When gases given off by factories and cars stay in the air above the earth, heat

Even a one- or two-degree difference in the temperature of the earth can cause changes in the climate.

cannot escape. Most scientists say that this is warming the earth and causing rapid climate change. Some animals will have to move to cooler places if they can. Other species will simply die out. Ice in the Arctic is melting so quickly that polar bears have to swim farther to catch seals. Polar bears don't have any other place to live—they can't move somewhere cooler.

Hunting and Poaching

Many countries have laws to protect certain animals and plants. *Poachers* break these laws and make money by killing and capturing certain animals or digging up plants.

Illegal hunting for sport is also reducing the numbers of many animals.

In Africa, poachers kill elephants for the ivory from their tusks. The black rhinoceros is also at great risk because of a false belief that its horn cures cancer.

20

People are even stealing black rhinoceros horns from museums! An organization has been airlifting black rhinos to secret areas that are safer from poachers.

New Species
People often spoil habitats by bringing new species to places where they don't

Eco comes from a Greek word meaning home.

normally live. This upsets the balance of an *ecosystem*. An ecosystem is all the living things and the place where they live together. Many rivers, lakes, and ponds are having problems because new species of fish or plants have taken over and are endangering the species already living there.

Threats for All Species
Habitat destruction
Pollution and climate change
Hunting and poaching
New species in an ecosystem

To conserve means to protect and save. People who protect the environment are called conservationists.

Help for Endangered Species
Many people are working to help endangered species and to *conserve* their habitats. Most of them do this by finding

22

ways to save the habitats where animals and plants live. Some do this by learning more about living things and what kind of habitats they need. Others help by setting up parks and nature reserves that protect the plants and animals living there.

Pandas and other endangered species cannot survive without human help. We all need to be conservationists!

Volunteers clean seabirds after the oil spill off the coast of New Orleans in 2010.

Whooping It Up

Scientists at the Patuxent Wildlife Research Center in Maryland are working to save whooping cranes. These big white birds are one of the most endangered kinds of crane in the world.

The scientists don't want the chicks they raise to get too used to people. To prepare the birds for life in the wild, workers wear long white robes and hoods. Whenever the workers feed the chicks or take them for a swim, they lead them around with a puppet on a stick that looks like a crane's head.

When the chicks are ready to fly, ultralight aircraft with pilots also dressed in robes guide the young cranes on their first trip to their winter feeding grounds in Florida. The trip is over 1,200 miles and can take two months!

2

China's National Treasures

For at least 3,000 years, the Chinese have written stories and poems about giant pandas. Ancient writings say that emperors kept these bears as a sign of wealth. A giant panda's skull was found in the tomb of an empress who lived over 2,000 years ago. Skins and bones of pandas have been discovered in older tombs as well. Today pandas are China's national symbol of peace and friendship.

Pandas have been around for over 3 million years!

World of the Giant Panda

All the forests of southern and eastern China were once the home of pandas. Now they live in the south-central mountains of the Sichuan, Shaanxi, and Gansu provinces. The Chinese government has set up nature

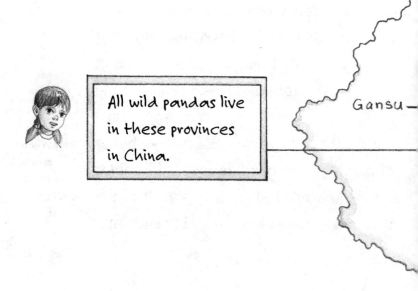

All wild pandas live in these provinces in China.

Gansu—

reserves in these mountains to protect pandas and other species of plants and animals.

Mist and clouds drift over the mountains there. Heavy rains fall on the trees and the thick groves of bamboo covering the slopes.

A number of plants and animals that live here are also endangered.

These ancient, lonely mountains are the home of all the wild giant pandas, as well as rare and interesting animals such as blood pheasants, bamboo rats, and even another bear—the Asiatic black bear.

Clouded leopards with spots shaped like clouds, golden snub-nosed monkeys with pale blue faces, and red pandas, which look like raccoons, hide in the tall trees.

Red pandas are also a threatened species. They are not related to giant pandas.

Giant Bear Cats

One of the Chinese names for *panda* is *giant bear cat*. At one time, people thought that pandas were in the raccoon family. Recently scientists discovered that pandas are a unique species of bear. Even though pandas are in the bear family, they're different in many ways from other bears.

Pandas don't have round eyes. Their pupils are vertical (straight up and down) like a cat's eye. That's one reason for that Chinese name.

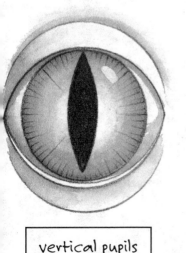

vertical pupils

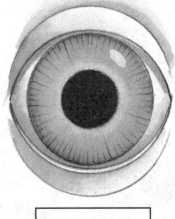

round pupils

Most bears are *omnivores*, eating both plants and meat. But pandas are a grass-eating bear. Almost all of their diet comes from bamboo.

Most bears hibernate in the winter, when food is hard to find. Bamboo grows all winter long. Pandas don't store fat in their

Pandas usually sleep twelve to fourteen hours a day.

bodies like many other bears. They must have food all the time.

During the winter, pandas move lower down the mountains, where it's warmer. Their thick woolly coats have two layers of fur. They stay warm even in the snow.

Giant pandas have five toes with claws, plus a long wrist bone that acts like an *opposable* thumb. An opposable thumb can move in different directions and pick up things. Apes, humans, and a few other animals have opposable thumbs.

Possums have opposable thumbs on their back feet.

Panda Ways

Like most bears, giant pandas don't live in groups. Giant pandas might share the same groves of bamboo, but they usually only get together to mate.

When pandas feel threatened, they

bob their heads, stare, and growl. They also might hit with their front paws, lunge forward, or bite.

To show they don't want to fight, pandas cover their eyes and muzzles with their paws and turn their heads.

Wild pandas don't travel far. Their bodies are thick and heavy. Because bamboo forests are so dense, the bears are not built to run in short bursts of speed like many other bears.

Although pandas live on the ground, they're also comfortable in trees. They climb up to sun themselves, take naps, and escape predators.

Pandas use their sharp claws to climb trees.

Panda Noises

Pandas communicate with a variety of bleats, barks, and honks. Adult pandas woo their mates with special noises during mating season. Sometimes they sound like a bleating goat, or they make a sort of huffing noise.

A Special Diet

In the wild, the giant pandas' diet is 99 percent bamboo. When they eat, they sit on the ground with their feet stretched out in front, much like a human sits.

Giant pandas have been known to spend up to sixteen hours a day eating. They eat thirty to forty pounds of food in one day!

The reason that pandas eat so much is that bamboo doesn't have many *nutrients*

That's about ten times as much as an average person eats each day!

Pandas in the wild eat forty-two different species of bamboo.

(NOO-tree-intz). They need to consume a lot. Bamboo is also hard to digest and passes through their bodies very quickly.

Nutrients are the vitamins, minerals, and proteins needed to be healthy.

37

 Bamboo is about 90 percent water, but pandas still drink from streams. They also sit in them to cool off.

Pandas love to feast on the first sweet sprouts of bamboo, but they eat all of the plant—the leaves, shoot, and roots.

Bamboo is hard to chew. Pandas have strong jaws, and their back teeth are flat like those of cattle or goats. These teeth crush and grind the bamboo. Their front, sharper teeth bite through the tough stalks. Pandas have a strong bite, stronger than a lion or tiger!

The San Diego Zoo treated two-year-old Yun Zi to a birthday cake made of bamboo leaves and colored pieces of ice.

Pandas in zoos also eat bamboo, but they eat other things as well. Their keepers feed them carrots, apples, sweet potatoes, and biscuits with lots of fiber.

Wild pandas will sometimes eat other grasses and roots or small rodents.

Pandas like to eat different kinds of bamboo, and they like certain parts of the bamboo at different times.

Today forest experts are planting different kinds of bamboo next to each other in panda reserves. They hope that when one species of bamboo dies, others will be there for the pandas to eat.

Life Span

Pandas in the wild might live for twenty years. Pandas live longer in zoos. Hsing Hsing was twenty-eight when he died at the National Zoo. In China, pandas in zoos have lived to be even older.

Earthquake!

The Wolong National Nature Reserve in China is a protected area for giant pandas and many other endangered species. Wildlife experts built a center there to study and breed pandas. More than sixty panda cubs have been born at Wolong.

On May 12, 2008, the ground at the reserve suddenly began to shake like jelly. Rocks as big as cars flew into the air, and mudslides roared down the mountains. The Wolong Reserve was only a few miles from the epicenter of a huge earthquake!

The quake destroyed roads, precious bamboo groves, and the panda houses. When it was over, workers found the pandas in trees, shaking and gripping the branches with all their might. Five workers on the reserve and one panda at the research center lost their lives.

Word of the disaster spread quickly. People all over the world, including many schoolchildren, sent money to rebuild the center. Today pandas from the research center are living in other reserves until Wolong is ready for their return.

3

Starting Small

When giant pandas are between four and eight years old, they begin to mate. The mating season usually starts in the spring. To attract a mate, pandas make noises and leave scent markers on bushes and trees. Sometimes the males fight one another over a female. Sometimes the males chase the females up and down trees.

Pandas usually give birth from

Each female has only two or three days during the mating season when she can get pregnant.

summer into fall. Most females have cubs every two years.

To prepare for her cub, the mother makes a den in a hollow tree or cave. She might have two cubs, but usually only one survives.

In her lifetime, a female panda might raise five to eight cubs.

New Babies

It's really amazing that baby pandas survive at all. They are among the most helpless creatures in the world. A newborn is about six inches long and weighs only three to five ounces.

The babies are very weak and can't move by themselves. They are born pink and blind, with a slight covering of white hair. In a little over a week, dark patches appear on their skin where the fur will be black.

A newborn panda is about as long as a pencil and as light as a stick of butter!

Because a cub doesn't have much fur, it depends on its mother for warmth. For a few weeks, the baby never leaves the mother's body. Panda mothers do a good job of feeding and cleaning their helpless babies.

The mother must be careful when she and her cub sleep. Pandas have been known to roll over on their babies and crush them.

When she moves around, a mother panda always carries her cub in her mouth, not in her paws.

There are over 5,000 kinds of mammals, including humans.

Like humans, pandas are *mammals*. Mammals are warm-blooded animals with hair and backbones, and they nurse their young with their own milk.

The mother's milk is high in fat. A cub usually gains ten times its birth weight in

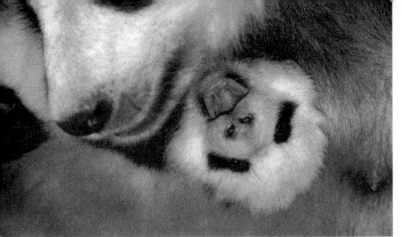

Baby pandas squall loudly almost all the time until about two months after they're born.

only five to six weeks. The cub might nurse as often as fourteen times a day.

Because the mothers can't leave their babies, they go without food for as long as twenty-five days. After three or four weeks, the cub can stay warm on its own. Now the mother will leave to find her first meal since the baby arrived. (And get away from all that noise!)

 Unlike pandas in the wild, baby pandas at the Conservation and Research Center for the Giant Panda in Wolong have a chance to play together.

Growing Up Fast

When the cub is about six weeks old, its eyes begin to open, and it quiets down. It starts to look more like a real panda and spends less time nursing. After about two months, the cub begins crawling. Its eyes are fully open at three months, and it also begins to toddle around and play.

At five months, the cub is up and running—sort of. At this age, it's very clumsy. It rolls around, falls, or does somersaults trying to keep up with its mother. Later, the cub will have a waddling walk like all adult pandas.

A mother panda will often leave her cub for a day or two to find food. Trees are safe places for the cub to hide out and wait for her.

Imagine growing from the weight of a stick of butter to my weight in just one year!

At about three months, teeth start to come in. But it's not until the cubs are between five and six months old that they start eating bamboo. When the cubs are a year old, they can weigh from fifty to seventy-five pounds!

Male pandas can reach 250 pounds and female pandas about 220.

Mothers and their cubs usually stay together until the cubs are about two or three years old. The young bears continue to grow until they are about five. When the bears are fully grown, they'll be about the size of an American black bear.

They'll also have large heads, thick bodies, and round ears. Adult pandas measure about two or three feet tall at their shoulders when they're standing on four legs. Their bodies are from four to six feet long. It's hard to believe that just five years ago, these same pandas were as tiny as mice!

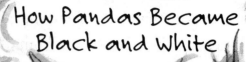

How Pandas Became Black and White

There's an ancient Tibetan myth about how pandas became black and white. The story says that pandas were once all white. Then one day, a panda and her cub began playing with a young shepherd girl. Suddenly a leopard crept up and attacked them. The girl died defending her panda friends.

All the pandas mourned by putting ashes on their paws and arms. As their tears fell, they wiped them away. They covered their ears to drown out the crying of the other bears. Then they hugged one another. Everywhere they put their paws turned black from the ashes.

No one knows for sure why pandas are black and white. It's likely that their coloring helps them hide in the dark woods and snow. They are especially hard to find when they climb a tree.

4

Endangered Species

It's difficult to give the total number of endangered species because many have yet to be discovered. It's estimated that there are almost 10,000 endangered species of plants and animals and another 10,000 that are at risk. The list includes everything from beautiful Fender's blue butterflies to Steller sea lions, which can reach over 2,000 pounds!

Overfishing has caused many ocean species to become endangered and almost extinct. Coral reefs are dying off in record numbers due to climate change and pollution. Until recent years, we knew more about the surface of the moon than the depths of the ocean.

Strange and Wonderful

Many people know about endangered animals such as tigers, elephants, and whales. But there are also wonderful animals that few people have ever heard of.

There's an endangered bat that lives on only a few islands in the Pacific Ocean. The Mariana fruit bat is considered to be a delicacy, so it is illegally hunted and eaten by humans.

There are about 10,000 bird species; 600 are endangered.

There are endangered penguins in New

Zealand with glowing yellow eyes called yellow-eyed penguins. Because the coastal forests where they nest are being cleared, their habitat is disappearing, and, sadly, so are they.

These yellow-eyed penguins are headed to their nest in the thick grass.

Most salamanders look like small lizards. They are actually amphibians (am-FIB-ee-unz) and belong to a group that includes frogs, toads, and newts.

About 30 to 50 percent of all amphibians, like the Chinese giant salamander, are threatened with extinction.

There's a salamander in China that can grow up to six feet long and makes a sound like an infant crying! The Chinese call it the baby fish. Other people call it the Chinese giant salamander.

The salamanders are dying out from habitat loss, from pollution, and from being used in Chinese medicine. The Chinese also think they're very good to eat!

Maybe the hooded seals of the Arctic should be called balloon seals. The males are amazing. When they get angry, they inflate a sac between their eyes that is a foot or more wide! They also blow up a bright red nasal balloon through their nostrils!

 Male hooded seals fight on the Magdalen Islands in Canada.

Warmer temperatures in the Arctic are putting these interesting creatures at risk. They aren't endangered yet, but their numbers are declining, and they might someday be in danger of extinction.

Let's go meet some other wonderful species that need our help!

Bengal Tigers

The Bengal tigers of India are beautiful animals. Sadly, fewer than 2,500 exist today. Some live in mangrove swamps or in steamy rain forests. Others make their homes in snowy forests.

Bengals roar so loudly that they can be heard up to two miles away! Some weigh as much as 500 pounds. When they run, tigers can reach speeds of up to 35 miles per hour. Maybe that's why a group of tigers is called a streak!

Bengal tigers track their prey at night. They prefer large animals like deer, wild pigs, buffalo, and even crocodiles or bears.

Bengal tigers have beautiful striped coats. No two look exactly the same. If you shave a Bengal tiger, the stripes still show up on its skin! Bengal tigers are protected, but they continue to be hunted as trophies, for their skins, and for use in Chinese medicine.

Fender's Blue Butterflies and Kincaid's Lupines

The Fender's blue butterfly is found only in the Willamette Valley in Oregon. This beautiful, small butterfly has just a one-inch wingspan. It was discovered in the 1920s, and then seemed to disappear forever. In 1989, someone found small groups of the butterflies that still existed.

Fender's blue butterflies depend on a wildflower called Kincaid's lupine. They lay their eggs on these plants. When caterpillars hatch from the eggs, they eat the lupine leaves. Then the caterpillars change into butterflies that live only a week to ten days. Before they die, the Fender's blue butterflies mate and lay new eggs on the lupine. The cycle starts all over again.

The problem is that Kincaid's lupine is

badly endangered because of habitat loss. If the lupine dies out, so do the butterflies. Scientists from the Oregon Zoo in Portland are collecting its seeds in hopes of saving the lupine . . . and saving the Fender's blue butterfly as well.

Orangutans

Orangutans come from the forests of Borneo and Sumatra. They are large apes with long arms and bodies covered with reddish hair. Orangutans can live up to sixty years in captivity.

Orangutans have opposable thumbs. They use tools such as sticks to trap insects or find ropes and vines to make swings and hammocks.

They also turn leaves into cups for water and make umbrellas by holding big leaves over their heads when it rains. When insects buzz around their heads, they swat them with leafy fly swatters.

Bonnie, an orangutan at the National Zoo, imitates her keepers. She sweeps her enclosure and cleans the windows (with dirty rags). She's even learned to whistle just by watching them! Everyone agrees that orangutans are really smart animals. Habitat loss and poaching have put them in grave danger.

Sloths

Sloths spend most of their time upside down in the trees of Central and South America. They eat leaves and sleep hanging from branches with their sharp claws. Sloths sleep up to eighteen hours a day.

Sloths don't move a lot, but when they need to escape from a predator, they can actually be pretty fast. They are also good swimmers.

Sloths have blue-green algae growing on their fur. This helps these slow-moving animals blend in with the trees to hide from their predators. The algae also serves as food for some species of insects, including beetles and little moths. Each sloth is its own little ecosystem! Sloths are in danger because of poaching and because people are cutting down the forests where they live.

Kiwis

Kiwis are very unusual birds from New Zealand. They are about the size of chickens. Even though they're birds, they can't fly. They have a face full of whiskers. Their shaggy feathers look like hair and feel like fur!

Most birds depend on their eyesight. Kiwis don't see well. Instead, they rely on their senses of smell and hearing. They are the only birds that have nostrils at the end of their beaks. They lift them up all the time to sniff the air for food or predators, just like dogs!

Kiwis usually mate for life and can live for up to forty years. But settlers brought dogs, cats, and ferrets to New Zealand, which are hunting kiwis into extinction.

Sea Otters

Sea otters are native to the coasts of California, Alaska, Russia, and Japan. They are about four feet long with webbed back feet.

Sea otters hunt for crabs, clams, mussels, and fish. When they find food, they tuck it under their armpits and swim to the surface. They also bring up rocks that they use as tools to break open crab and abalone shells.

The otters float on their backs and rest the rocks on their stomachs. Then they hold the shells between their paws and pound them on the rocks until they crack open.

Sea otters sleep on their backs. To keep their sleeping cubs from floating away, they wrap kelp around them to anchor them down.

Otters have the thickest fur of any animal—about one million hairs per square inch! Their fur traps in heat. They must groom themselves all the time to stay clean and waterproof. If oil or dirt gets on their fur, they can die from heat loss. Fishing nets, pollution, and oil spills are very harmful to this species.

Snow Leopards

Some people call snow leopards mountain ghosts. That's because very few people have ever seen one in the wild. These shy cats live high in the snowy mountains of central Asia. Their soft gray coats make them hard to spot among cliffs and rocks.

Compared to other big cats, snow leopards aren't very large. They weigh up to 120 pounds. They feed on wild sheep and goats.

Snow leopards have the longest tails of any cat. Their tails are almost as long as their bodies. When they sleep they curl them around themselves for warmth. Their tails also help them keep their balance when they spring out to catch prey. Snow leopards can leap over thirty feet. That's about six times longer than their bodies!

Snow leopards are in danger because poachers kill them for their beautiful fur and for use in traditional Chinese medicine.

5

🐼

Two Heroes

As a little girl in England, Jane Goodall dreamed of studying animals. It all started when Jane was a baby, and her father gave her a toy chimpanzee for Christmas. She named it Jubilee, after a chimp in the London Zoo. She carried it everywhere. All through her childhood, Jane loved animals and was curious about them.

When she was three, her mother found her waiting for a hen to lay eggs. The little

Jane says her dog Rusty taught her a lot about animals.

girl sat quietly for five hours until the hen produced one egg! As she got older, Jane read everything she could about animals. She decided at an early age that learning about the animals of Africa would be her life's work.

Off to Africa

When Jane was twenty-six, she set off for Africa. In Kenya she met Dr. Louis Leakey. He and his wife were famous scientists who'd discovered fossils of the earliest humans. Dr. Leakey became her

Jane Goodall and Louis Leakey

mentor. He asked Jane to help him by studying wild chimpanzees in what is now the Gombe National Park in Tanzania.

Jane and the Chimpanzees

Jane had no training to study animals of any kind. But she had spirit and courage. She left for the park on the eastern shore of Lake Tanganyika (tan-gahn-YEEK-uh). The park is lush with beautiful green hills, dense forests, and steep valleys.

Lake Tanganyika is the longest freshwater lake in the world. It is surrounded by four African countries!

Jane set up camp and got to work. For months she tracked the same group of chimpanzees. Because they were uneasy when Jane came too close, she sat for days watching them from a distance with her binoculars.

It wasn't easy. For much of the time, she lived alone in a jungle forest with bloodsucking leeches, prowling leopards, biting insects, dangerous snakes, wandering buffalo, and rivers full of crocodiles! Jane got very sick twice from malaria, and she went for long periods of time without speaking to another human being. But Jane's patience finally paid off. At last, a chimpanzee that she'd named David Greybeard crept up to her camp. He reached for a banana and quickly left. The next day, he brought other chimpanzees with him to get more bananas.

One day, Jane found David Greybeard sitting alone. She sat down next to him and offered him a leaf. He dropped it, but then gently squeezed her hand. David Greybeard became Jane's closest link to the other chimpanzees. After he accepted her, she was finally allowed to sit among them as they went about their daily life.

Even though David Greybeard wasn't one of their leaders, the other chimps seemed to love and respect him.

Jane spent years studying this same group of chimpanzees. She learned that though they often treated one another with love and support, they could also hold grudges, fight, and even kill each other.

 Chimpanzees are suffering from habitat destruction, poaching, and diseases.

When she saw David Greybeard use a stick to catch termites, Jane realized that chimpanzees used tools. No one had ever known this before.

When any chimpanzee died, Jane felt as if she'd lost a friend. The hardest death of all was that of David Greybeard. She mourned for him as she'd done for no other animal.

David Greybeard died of pneumonia in 1968.

Jane created the Gombe Stream Research Center for the conservation of chimpanzees. She married and had a son there. Jane's work became so well known that research students came from all over the world to study with her.

It's been fifty years since Jane first went to Africa. Since then, she's written books about her adventures and received many honors for her work.

At Dr. Leakey's urging, Jane took time off to go to an English university to learn more about animals.

Jane speaks to Congress about the need for greater cooperation among nations in protecting the planet.

Jane Today

Jane Goodall travels around the world giving talks about saving endangered species. Jane has never stopped working to save her beloved chimpanzees. In spite of her work, the chimpanzees' habitat is still shrinking. Jane created the Jane Goodall Institute, with branches all over the world, to teach about conservation. She also formed a group called Roots and Shoots that is just for young people.

When Jane returns to the Gombe, she says that she feels a powerful sense of peace.

Jane still has Jubilee. It sits on her dresser in England.

George Schaller

In 1947, when George Schaller was fourteen, his family moved from Germany to the United States. George's mother told him he could take only one thing from his home there. George very carefully packed up a special bird's nest he'd found with different-colored eggs in it. Even as a child, he loved animals and dreamed of studying them in faraway places.

George Schaller became a wildlife biologist. His first job was to study mountain gorillas in the Virunga chain of volcanoes in Africa. Mountain gorillas are the rarest and most endangered of all gorillas.

At that time no one knew much about them. Many people thought that gorillas were fierce and dangerous animals. George discovered that they are not dangerous at all. Instead, he found that gorillas are peaceful, gentle, and smart.

Like Jane, George researched animals by watching them for hours and writing down what he saw.

To avoid violence, males stage mock fights. They grab leaves and stuff them in their mouths. They stand up, throw plants, stamp their feet, and pound their

The largest males can weigh up to 500 pounds!

chests. If that's not enough, they'll drop down on all fours and run around like crazy, pretending to attack. Even with all of this, they rarely ever really fight.

Adult males are called silverbacks because of the gray hairs on their backs. One always leads the group.

George took notes as the gorillas played, hugged one another, or threw things around when they were upset. He noticed that they're afraid of snakes and don't like the water. (They can't swim.)

Baby gorillas are scared to death of caterpillars.

After two years, George came away with a deep love for these animals. His time with the gorillas changed his life forever.

 George is one of the few people to have ever seen a snow leopard in Nepal.

George became one of the first leaders in wildlife conservation.

Where's George?

George could be anywhere! For fifty years, he's lived all over the world studying animals. He and his wife and two young sons lived in the Serengeti in Africa while he researched lions. Some nights, lions would roar outside the family's tent. They

even came close enough to trip over the ropes of the tent!

George has gone to Brazil to learn about alligators, jaguars, and other animals. He was shot at in Afghanistan looking for Marco Polo sheep and was almost killed by poachers in Africa.

George and the Giant Pandas

In 1980, George wanted to find out why pandas were disappearing. Pandas were so popular that poachers were capturing them to sell as pets or to zoos. They also killed them for their pelts. George decided that at this time poaching was the pandas' biggest problem. His studies at the panda reserves helped George become one of the world's experts on giant pandas.

George has started conservation

The penalty for poaching pandas can be many years in prison.

efforts in the Amazon, Alaska, and Nepal. Because of his love for mountain gorillas, he helped create the Virunga National Park. It's the first park ever set aside for the conservation of mountain gorillas.

George Schaller and Jane Goodall have devoted their lives to saving endangered animals. Their work and the risks they've taken for animals have made both of them true heroes.

Turn the page to read about a Hollywood gorilla!

King Kong

Hollywood movies helped to create the myth that gorillas are terrifying animals. It all began in 1933 with the first *King Kong* movie. Since then the movie has been remade two more times. In the films, King Kong is a fifty-foot gorilla who escapes when he's brought from the wild to New York City.

In the last scene, King Kong climbs up the Empire State Building to get away from his captors. He's so dangerous and wild that fighter planes arrive and shoot him down.

After he's dead, people in the movie begin to realize that King Kong wasn't a monster; he was really a peaceful animal forced to defend himself.

King Kong led some people to believe that gorillas are brutal and fierce. In real life, we know that it doesn't take fighter planes to kill a gorilla. A single poacher is enough.

6

Hope for the Future

Even with the bad news, there's still hope. Today countries everywhere are making laws and setting aside land to protect living things.

Five countries in southern Africa have announced that they are joining fourteen national parks and nature reserves into a single area as big as France to protect the species that live there.

The nature reserve will be named the

Okavango-Zambezi Conservation Zone. This zone will protect more than 250,000 elephants, along with other endangered animals like cheetahs, rhinoceroses, and African wild dogs.

Coming Back

Endangered species can be saved from extinction. Gray wolves were once endangered and now they're not, and the same is true of American bald eagles, peregrine falcons, and gray whales.

Jane Goodall carries a California condor's feather wherever she goes as a sign of hope. Condors are the largest flying land birds, with wingspans of over nine feet! They fly at speeds of fifty-five miles per hour and up to 15,000 feet high in the air! Some American Indians called condors thunderbirds and created a myth that their huge wings created thunder.

In the 1980s, only twenty-two California condors remained. They were becoming extinct because of poaching and lead poisoning and habitat destruction. Then the San Diego Zoo stepped in and created a breeding program. Today over 200 live in the wild.

California condors clean things up by eating dead animals. They can live up to sixty years!

Kids Can!

Jane Goodall believes that doing small things every day makes a big difference. Kids can help. First they can learn about the natural world. They can build bird feeders, pick up litter, and ask their parents not to use harmful chemicals in their yards.

To save energy, kids can turn off the lights they're not using, bicycle instead of going everywhere in a car, and recycle! Kids can think before they waste paper or buy water in plastic bottles.

Kids can take care of their pets. They can keep their cats inside so they don't kill birds, and make sure their dogs and cats have rabies shots.

All of us can do something to make the world a better place for all living things. Let's get started right now!

Doing More Research

There's a lot more you can learn about pandas and other endangered species. The fun of research is seeing how many different sources you can explore.

Books

Most libraries and bookstores have books about endangered species.

Here are some things to remember when you're using books for research:

1. You don't have to read the whole book. Check the table of contents and the index to find the topics you're interested in.

2. Write down the name of the book.

When you take notes, make sure you write down the name of the book in your notebook so you can find it again.

3. Never copy exactly from a book.

When you learn something new from a book, put it in your own words.

4. Make sure the book is <u>nonfiction</u>.

Some books tell make-believe stories about endangered species. Make-believe stories are called *fiction*. They're fun to read, but not good for research.

Research books have facts and tell true stories. They are called *nonfiction*. A librarian or teacher can help you make sure the books you use for research are nonfiction.

Here are some good nonfiction books about pandas and other endangered species:

- *Can We Save Them?* by David Dobson

- *Endangered Animals*, a DK Eyewitness Book, by Ben Hoare and Tom Jackson

- *Endangered Pandas*, Earth's Endangered Animals series, by John Crossingham and Bobbie Kalman

- *Giant Pandas* by Gail Gibbons

- *Pandas*, A National Geographic Kids Reader, by Anne Schreiber

- *The Remarkable Rainforest: An Active-Learning Book for Kids* by Toni Albert

Museums and Zoos

Many museums and zoos have exhibits on pandas and other endangered species. These places can help you learn more about endangered animals.

When you go to a museum or zoo:

1. Be sure to take your notebook!
Write down anything that catches your interest. Draw pictures, too!

2. Ask questions.
There are almost always people at museums and zoos who can help you find what you're looking for.

3. Check the calendar.
Many museums and zoos have special events and activities just for kids!

Here are some museums and zoos
with exhibits about pandas and other
endangered species:

- American Museum of Natural History
  (New York)

- Bronx Zoo (New York)

- Fort Worth Zoo (Texas)

- National Zoo (Washington, D.C.)

- Natural History Museum of Los Angeles

- San Diego Zoo

DVDs

There are some great nonfiction DVDs about pandas and other endangered species. As with books, make sure the DVDs you watch for research are nonfiction!

Check your library or video store for these and other nonfiction titles about endangered animals:

- *African Cats*
  from Disneynature

- *Kids @ Discovery: Endangered Species!*
  from Cerebellum Corporation

- *Mountain Gorilla*
  from National Geographic IMAX Experience

- *Secrets of the Wild Panda,*
  Young Explorers series
  from National Geographic

The Internet

Many websites have facts about pandas and other endangered species. Some also have games and activities that can help make learning about endangered animals even more fun.

Ask your teacher or your parents to help you find more websites like these:

- animal.discovery.com/guides /endangered/endangered.html

- animals.nationalgeographic.com/animals /mammals/snow-leopard

- enchantedlearning.com/subjects /rainforest

- kids.nationalgeographic.com/kids /animals/creaturefeature/panda

- kids.sandiegozoo.org/animals/mammals /giant-panda

- kidsplanet.org

- library.thinkquest.org/06aug/00442
  /orangutans.html

- nationalzoo.si.edu/Animals/GiantPandas
  /PandaFacts

Good luck!

Index

Photographs courtesy of:

Have you read the adventure that matches up with this book?

Don't miss Magic Tree House® #48

A Perfect Time for Pandas

The magic tree house whisks Jack and Annie away to a village in the mountains of Southwest China, close to a world-famous panda reserve. But they've arrived on the day of a terrible earthquake! Will they be able to rescue the pandas?

If you're looking forward to
Magic Tree House® #49: *Stallion by Starlight,*
you'll love finding out the facts
behind the fiction in

Magic Tree House®
Fact Tracker

HORSE HEROES

A nonfiction companion to
Magic Tree House® #49:
Stallion by Starlight

It's Jack and Annie's very own guide
to horse heroes.

Coming in March 2013!

Magic Tree House® Books

Magic Tree House® Fact Trackers

More Magic Tree House®

SAL MURDOCCA is best known for his amazing work on the Magic Tree House® series. He has written and/or illustrated over two hundred children's books, including *Dancing Granny* by Elizabeth Winthrop, *Double Trouble in Walla Walla* by Andrew Clements, and *Big Numbers* by Edward Packard. He has taught writing and illustration at the Parsons School of Design in New York. He is the librettist for a children's opera and has recently completed his second short film. Sal Murdocca is an avid runner, hiker, and bicyclist. He has often bicycle-toured in Europe and has had many one-man shows of his paintings from these trips. He lives and works with his wife, Nancy, in New City, New York.